Secrets to Give your Kids Great Science Education

PRAISE
of the Book

"A book of great inspiration, courage, and hope, every word rings with truth, kindness, and the beauty of the human spirit."

— Greenman Vijaypal Baghel
Renowned Environmentalist/Honored as Social Reformers of India by Wikipedia

"This is an audacious and powerful read! This suggests us great parenting style which can mould children for great nation."

— Dr. VK Goswami
Visiting Scientist; UNIDO, ICTP, ITALY, Expert Panel, NOAA, UNV, ICAO & AIU Rosters Vice Chancellor

"What a beautiful, rich, and wise book on parenting. I wish I could give a copy to every new parent on the planet."

— Dinesh Verma

Author & CEO, Pendown Press

This book is selected by National Book Trust(NBT), Government of India at:

- **Cape Town Book Fair (Sourth Africa), 2012**
- **Sharjah International Book Fair (UAE), 2013**

SECRETS
TO GIVE
YOUR KIDS
GREAT
SCIENCE
EDUCATION
How science book becomes interesting
if it is made like this book
Worldwide Published by
Pendown Press

PENDOWN PRESS

An ISO 9001 & ISO 14001 Certified Co.,

Regd. Office: 2525/193, 1st Floor, Onkar Nagar-A,
Tri Nagar, Delhi-110035
Ph.: 09350849407, 09312235086
E-mail: info@pendownpress.com
Branch Office: 1A/2A, 20, Hari Sadan, Ansari Road,
Daryaganj, New Delhi-110002
Ph.: 011-45794768
Website: PendownPress.com

First Edition: 2019
Price: ₹259/-
ISBN: 978-93-81970-02-7

Layout and Cover Designed by Pendown Graphics Team
Printed and Bound in India by Thomson Press India Ltd.

Contents

Few Words

Not all kids like all subjects, but it seems that science is the hardest for ordinary kids to get interested in. This could be because that a lot of parents themselves are not interested in science and kids seem to pick up on that. Teachers try everything that they can think of to make their subjects interesting and most of the time it works. Teachers who have passion for their subject are a lot more effective in getting kids interested in a subject than teachers who just sit and lecture a student.

As a parent you might be wondering how you can get your child interested in science. The first step is to become active and interested in what your child is doing. This is probably the most important thing you can do to get your child interested in anything. By showing your child that you are interested in what they are doing makes you child feel like they are doing something worthwhile. Because they are feeling important they will approach science with a new zest for learning.

Science does not have to be boring; by taking the time to answer your child's question or by having they answer their own question you are teaching them about science. Buying them that butterfly habitat is also teaching them about science. And the best news is it is all fun and interesting for them.

– Dinesh Verma

Acknowledgements

I acknowledge the almighty GOD or universal energy which has brought precious words of wisdom in front of my eyes, the wisdom to touch the soul of those words and creativity to present some of them to parent in YOU.

Out of the large repository of words few words I would like to acknowledge:

When I first helped my newborn son, I looked at him with tenderness and wondered and thought to myself, you are the most precious gift from God. I don't own you. I am here to help you find your way, to love you, and to let you go.

Susie Risho, Mother of Three Grown Boys

And I am a practising parent trying to touch the soul of above words.

I would like to put in my appreciation and acknowledgement for my family members, relatives, friends and Team of Pendown Press and PendownPress.com.

I convey my special thanks to all the kids with whom we experimented and played activities and all those who entertained and taught me.

No work can find success without the most important part, that is, YOU, The READERS. I wholeheartedly thank all those who took pain in the making of the book.

-Dinesh Verma

1 INTRODUCTION

"The well-being and welfare of children
should always be our focus."
~ *Todd Tiahrt*

As a parent, you are preparing your child for a world vastly different from the one in which you grew up. Our increasingly technological society will need citizens who have received far more advanced instruction in science and technology than most of us received when we were in school. Even children who don't want to become physicists, engineers or computer technicians will need some knowledge of science and technology just to conduct their everyday lives. Every citizen needs to be scientifically literate in order to make informed decisions about health, safety and citizenship. Our children need our help and guidance to prepare for the world that awaits them.

Scientific knowledge is cumulative: To learn new things, you must build on what you already know. So, its important that your child start learning early — at home. A good way for you to begin the learning process is by sharing your own interest in science. How you view and talk about science can influence your child's attitudes towards science — and how he/she approaches learning science. Do not undermine a child's interest and attitudes by saying things such as, "I was lousy in science, and I've done OK," or "I always hated science when I was in school. It's boring." Although you can't make your child like science, you can encourage him/her to do so, and you can help him/her to appreciate its value both in his/her everyday life and in preparing for his/her future.

In everyday interactions with your child, you can do many things and do them without lecturing or applying pressure to help him/her learn science. Here are a few ideas:

- See how long it takes for a sunflower or a rose to burst into full bloom.

- Watch the moon as it appears to change shape over the course of a month and record the changes.
- Look for constellations in the night sky.
- Bake a cake.
- Solve the problem of a drooping plant.
- Figure out how the spin cycle of the washing machine gets the water out of the clothes.
- Take apart an old clock or mechanical toy — you don't need to put it back together!
- Watch ice melt.
- Observe pigeons, squirrels, butterflies, ants or spider webs.
- Go for a walk and talk about how the dogs (or birds or cats) that you see are alike and different.
- Discover what materials the buildings in your community are made of. Wood? Concrete? Brick? Granite? Sandstone? Steel? Glass? Talk about the reasons for using these materials.

Learning to observe carefully is an important step leading to scientific explanations. Experiencing the world with your child and exchanging information with him/her about what you see are important too.

Finally, encourage your child to ask questions. If you can't answer all of his/her questions, that's all right — no one has all the answers, not even scientists. For example, point out that there's no known cure for a cold, but that we do know how diseases are passed from person to person — through germs. Some of the best answers you can give are, "What do you think?" and "Let's find out together." Together, you and your child can come to possible answers, test them out and check them by using reference books, the Internet, or by asking someone who is likely to know the correct answers.

How to Use this Book?

This book makes available to you information that you can use to help your child to learn science. It includes:

- Some basic information about science;
- Activities for you and your child to do, both in the home and the community;
- Practical suggestions for how to work with teachers and schools to help your child succeed in science.

xxx

History will judge us by the difference we make in the everyday lives of children.

-Nelson Mandela

2 THE BASICS

"You have to support your children to have a healthy relationship."
~ *Connie Sellecca*

Science gives the knowledge about the world based on facts learned through observation, scientific thinking and experiments. Children can pick up a habit of looking at a thing with the analytical bent of mind, if he is trained and encouraged to do so. A child seeking scientific explanation of a thing, occurrence or phenomenon will be able to be a good student of science if their parents prepare a favourable atmosphere for their learning.

What is Science?

Science is not just a collection of facts. Of course, facts are an important part of science: Water freezes at 0 degrees Celsius (or 32 degrees Fahrenheit), and the earth moves around the sun. But science is much, much more. Science involves:

- Observing what's happening;
- Classifying or organizing information;
- Predicting what will happen;
- Testing predictions under controlled conditions to see if they are correct; and
- Drawing conclusions.

Science involves trial and error — trying, failing and trying again. Science doesn't provide all the answers. It requires us to be skeptical so that our scientific "conclusions" can be modified or changed altogether as we make new discoveries.

Children have their Own "Scientific Concepts"

Very young children can come up with many interesting explanations to make sense of the world around them. When asked about the shape of the earth, for example, some will explain that the earth has to be flat because, if it were round like a ball, people and things would fall off it. Presented with a globe and told that this is the true shape of the earth, these children may adapt their explanation by saying that the earth is hollow and that people live on flat ground inside it.

Even older children can come up with unique "scientific" explanations, as in the following examples provided by middle-school students:

"Fossils are bones that animals are through wearing."

"Some people can tell what time it is by looking at the sun, but I've never been able to make out the numbers."

"Gravity is stronger on the earth than on the moon because here on earth we have a bigger mass."

"A blizzard is when it snows sideways."

Asking Questions

As mentioned earlier, it's important to encourage your child to ask questions. It's also important to ask your child questions that will get him/her talking about his/ her ideas and to listen carefully to his/her answers. Keep in mind that children's experiences help them form their ideas — ideas that may, or may not, match current scientific interpretations. Help your child to look at things in new ways. For instance, in regard to the blizzard, you could ask, "Have you ever seen it snow sideways?" or "What do you think causes it to snow sideways sometimes?"

Such conversation can be an important form of inquiry or learning. Encourage your child by letting him/her know that it's OK to make mistakes or admit he/she doesn't know something. Rather than saying, "No, that's wrong," when he/she gives an incorrect explanation, give him/her accurate information or help him/her to find it. Going back to the blizzard, you could ask your child, "How could you check your definition?" "How does the dictionary's definition of "blizzard" fit with what you said about snow moving sideways?"

Knowing that you are willing to listen will help your child to gain confidence in his/her own thinking and encourage his/her interest in science. And listening to what he/she says will help him/her to figure out what he/she knows and how he/she knows it.

Hands-on Works Well

Investigating and experimenting are great ways for children to learn science and increase their understanding of scientific ideas. Hands-on science can also help children think critically and gain confidence in their own ability to solve problems. Young children especially are engaged by things they can touch, manipulate and change; and by situations that allow them to figure out what happens — in short, events and puzzles that they can investigate, which is at the very heart of scientific study. While hands-on science works well, it can also be messy and time-consuming. So, before you get started, see what is involved in an activity — including how long it will take.

Less is More

It's tempting to try to teach children just a little about many different subjects. Although children can't possibly learn everything about science, they do need and will want to learn many facts. The best way to help them learn to think scientifically is to introduce them to just a few topics in depth.

Finding the Right Activity for your Child

Different children have different interests and will respond differently to science activities. A sand and rock collection that was a big hit with an 8-year-old daughter may not be a big hit with a 6-year-old son.

Fortunately, children whose interests vary greatly can find plenty of science activities that are fun. If your son/daughter loves to cook, let him/her observe how tea changes color when lemon is added or how vinegar curdles milk. **Knowing your child is the best way to find suitable activities** for him/her. Here are some tips:

- Encourage activities that are neither too hard nor too easy for your child. If in doubt, err on the easy side, because something too difficult may give him/her the idea that science itself is too hard. Adults often assume that children need spectacular demonstrations to learn science, but this isn't true.

- Consider your child's personality and social habits. Some projects are best done alone, others in a group; some require help, others require little or no adult supervision. **Solitary activities may bore some children, while group projects may not appeal to others.**
- Select activities that are appropriate for the place you live in. Clearly, a brightly lighted city isn't the best place for stargazing.
- Allow your child to help select the activities. If you don't know whether he/she would rather collect shells or plant daffodils, ask him/her. When he/she picks something he/she wants to do, he/she'll learn more and have a better time doing it.

xxx

The solution to every parenting problem starts with nine little words:
'I'm here.'
'I hear you.'
'How can I help?'

3 DEVELOPING YOUR CHILD'S SCIENTIFIC UNDERSTANDING

"Always kiss your children goodnight, even if they're already asleep."
~ *H. Jackson Brown, Jr.*

Undoubtedly, sciencetific thinking begins at home. A kid, raised in a science friendly home is encouraged to ask questions, watch science programs on TV & think analytically.

Unifying Concepts and Processes

Children can be introduced gradually to basic scientific concepts that will provide a framework for understanding and connecting many scientific facts and observations. In this book, we will focus on five concepts and processes taken from the national science education standards. You can easily introduce your child to the following five concepts through the activities in this book and many other simple science-related activities that you and your child can do at home or in the community.

1. Systems, Order and Organization

The natural world is so large and complicated that scientists break it down into smaller parts in order to study it in depth. These smaller units are called systems. Scientists look for patterns through which they can classify — or organize — things into systems. For instance, animals that have fur or hair are classified as mammals. When you encourage your child to gather and organize objects according to their size or color — for example, leaves or insects — you are helping prepare him/her to think in terms of systems. Furthermore, scientists believe that nature is understandable and predictable — that there is an order to it. For instance, low barometric pressure is often followed by storms. Challenging your child to make reasonable predictions such as this will further prepare him/her to look at the world in a scientific way.

2. Evidence, Models and Explanations

Scientists test the explanations they come up with, and the results of their tests are evidence on which to base their explanations. Sometimes they call their explanations "theories" or "models" or "hypotheses". Children can test their theories about the world too: Is it the baking soda that makes my pancakes thick? Can I make thicker pancakes with more soda?

3. Change, Constancy and Measurement

The natural world changes continually. Some objects change rapidly and some at a rate too slow for us to observe. You can encourage your child to look for changes by asking him/her to observe and talk about:

- What happens to breakfast cereal when we pour milk on it?
- What happens over time when a plant isn't watered or exposed to proper sunlight?
- What changes can be reversed? Once water is turned into ice cubes, can it be turned back into water? Yes. But if an apple is cut into slices, can the slices be changed back into the whole apple?

Children can observe change more carefully through measurement. Keeping a growth chart or making a graph of the temperature each day will give your child practice looking for differences and measuring them — and help him/her to understand how he/she'll need to use math skills in learning science.

4. Evolution and Equilibrium

It's hard for children to understand evolution (how

things change over time) and equilibrium (how things attain a steady and balanced state of being). During these early years, you can, however, talk about how things change over time and point them out to your child. For instance, show your child a series of photos of him/herself from birth to the present and talk about the many ways he/she's changed. And, you can talk about balance and the work it often takes to achieve it: Learning to ride a bicycle or walk with a book on his/her head are good examples.

5. Form and Function

One of the simplest themes in science is all around: The shape of a natural thing is almost always related to its function. Begin with man-made objects. Can your child guess the use of a thimble, a corkscrew, a phonograph record? When you are looking at animals, ask him questions such as: "What might those plates do on the stegosauros's back?" "What sort of habitat would a web-footed platypus like?" His best guess will almost always be correct.

Scientific Integrity

Science fiction writer Isaac Asimov describes science as a "way of thinking." It is a way to look at the world that involves special principles of conduct, and the early years of elementary school are a good time to start teaching children scientific ethics. We should help them understand how important it is to:

- observe carefully;
- record accurately;
- try to look for patterns in an objective, unbiased way;
- share their observations (or results) honestly and in a way that allows others to test what they've said;
- realize that they might make mistakes;
- respect curiosity; and
- stay open to criticism and change.

xxx

"If you are a parent, open doors to unknown directions to the child so he can explore. Don't make him afraid of the unknown, give his support."

~Osho

4

ACTIVITIES

"Parenthood remains the greatest single
preserve of the amateur."
~ *Alvin Toffler*

Children learn by doing, by trying new ideas and challenging old ones. This doesn't just happen in school. You can help your child learn by providing him/her with safe, interesting learning experiences in a supportive atmosphere.

The activities that follow are designed for you to use with your child at home and in the community. The activities are intended to show your child that science plays a part in many everyday activities and that it is used in many places and environments. They also show that learning science doesn't require expensive equipment and complicated experiments.

For each activity, you'll see a grade span — from pre-school through grade 5 — that suggests when children should be ready to try it. Of course, children don't always learn — or become interested in — the same things at the same time. And they don't suddenly stop enjoying one thing and start enjoying another just because they are a little older. You're the best judge of which activity your child is ready to try. For example, you may find that an activity listed for children in grades 1 or 2 works well with your pre-schooler. On the other hand, you might discover that the same activity may not interest your child until he/she is in grade 3 or 4. Feel free to make changes in an activity — shorten or lengthen it — to suit your child's interests and attention span.

Safety First

Read through each activity before you try it with your child. In particular, look for this sign: It highlights any activity that requires adult supervision, such as those that involve heat, chemicals or sharp instruments.

Also make sure that your child understands any safety precautions that may be necessary for these — or any — science activities. In particular, you should:

- teach your child not to taste anything without your supervision;
- insist that he/she wear goggles whenever something could splash, burn, or shatter and endanger his/her eyes;

- teach him/her to follow warnings on manufacturers' labels and instructions for toys and science kits;
- keep toxic or other dangerous substances out of the reach of your child;
- teach him/her what he/she can do to avoid accidents; and
- teach him/her what to do if an accident occurs.

In a highlighted text near the end of each activity are a few facts and explanations for reinforcement and further teaching. But exploring, questioning and having a good time are more important than memorizing facts.

Recording Results

Keeping records is an important part of science. It helps us remember what did (and didn't) work. Before starting the activities, give your child a notebook — a science journal — in which he/she can record his/her observations. Remember that seeing isn't the only way to observe. Sometimes we use other senses:

We hear, feel, smell or taste some things (of course, your child should be careful about what he/she tastes — and he/she shouldn't taste anything without your permission).

If your child cannot write yet, he/she can tell you what to write for him/her or draw pictures of what he/she sees. In addition, you may want to use a simple camera to help record observations.

As a parent, you can help your child learn in a way no one else can. That desire to learn is a key to your child's success. And, of course, enjoyment is an important motivator for learning. As you choose activities to use with your child, remember that helping him/her to learn doesn't mean that you can't laugh or that you have to be serious. In fact, you can teach your child a lot through play. We hope that you and your child enjoy these activities and that they inspire you to think of additional activities of your own.

xxx

"To the world you are one person, *but to your child* you are **THE WORLD!**"

Make their world beautiful
&
fill it with **LOVE**!

5 SCIENCE IN THE HOME

"My children are the reason I laugh, smile and want to get up every morning."
~Gena Lee Nolin

Your home is a great place for you to begin to explore science with your child. Incorporating science activities and language into familiar routines will show your child how science works in his/her everyday life and provide him/her with a safe environment to explore and experiment.

1. A Science Walk

Pre-school - Kindergarten

Even a walk around the yard can provide many opportunities to introduce children to scientific concepts and processes by helping them to gain the scientific habit of observing what's around them.

What Parents Need?

- A magnifying glass
- Science journal

What Can Parents Do?

- Take a walk outside with your child — around the yard, to the end of the block, in the park — anywhere that's convenient. Invite him/her to bring along his/her science journal and show him/her how to use a magnifying glass. As you walk, stop and — depending on the season — ask him/her to use the lens to examine things such as the following:
  - dirt
  - leaves (from the same tree, one on the ground and one on the tree)
  - a flower
  - snowflakes
  - icicles
  - bugs
  - a mud puddle
  - a rock

- Ask him/her to talk about what he/she observes.

  Ask, for example:

  - What's on each side of this leaf?
  - How is this leaf on the ground different from the one on the tree?
  - Are all the petals on this flower of the same size and color?
  - Are these snowflakes exactly alike? How are they different?
  - How many legs does this bug have?
  - How many colors can you see in this mud puddle?

- Other questions you might ask as he/she observes and examines things along the way include the following:

  - Is it smooth or rough?
  - Is it hard or soft?
  - Is it dry or wet?
  - Is it alive? How do you know?
  - What shape is it?

- Give your child two different kinds of rocks or flowers and ask him/her to tell you how they are alike and different.

- Make sure he/she records his/her observations, reactions, findings and opinions in his/her science journal. Drawing pictures and taking photos are good ways to record observations, and you can help him/her to write appropriate captions. Encourage him/her to share his/her journal with others and to talk about his/her experiences.

Observing closely is an important part of science, and tools such as a magnifying glass help scientists — even young ones — to observe, measure and do things that they otherwise could not do.

2. Breaking the Tension

Pre-school - Kindergarten

These simple activities demonstrate *surface tension.*

What Parents Need?

- Index card
- Safety scissors
- Sink filled with water
- Glass half filled with water
- Liquid dishwashing detergent
- Ground pepper
- Toothpicks

What Can Parents Do?

- From an index card, cut out a boat shape. Make the boat about 2.5 inches long and 1.5 inches wide. Have your child place the boat gently on the water in the sink. Have him/her pour a little detergent at the notch end of the boat. Ask him to describe what happens. (Note: To repeat this experiment, you'll need to use fresh water to make the boat move).

- Next, sprinkle a little ground pepper on the water in the glass. Give your child a toothpick and tell him/her to dip it in the middle of the pepper. Ask him/her what happens. Then tell him/her to put a drop of the detergent on another toothpick and dip it into the pepper. Now what happens?

Surface tension results when the hydrogen in water molecules stick to one another as well as to the water below them. This creates a strong but flexible film on the water's surface. The detergent disrupts the molecules and "breaks the tension," making the boat go forward and the pepper move to the sides of the glass.

3. Bubbles

Pre-school - Kindergarten

Children can learn more about surface tension and about change just by blowing bubbles!

What Parents Need?

- 8 tablespoons of dishwashing liquid
- 1 quart water
- 1 drinking straw
- A shallow pan

What Can Parents Do?

- Mix the dishwashing liquid with the water and pour it into the pan. Give your child a straw and tell him/her to blow through it as he/she moves it slowly across the surface of the solution. Ask him/her to notice the size of the bubbles that he/she makes.

- Next, have your child try to make a very big bubble that covers the surface of the pan. Have him/her do the following:
  - Dip one end of the straw into the solution. Then hold the straw slightly above the surface. Blow into it very gently. He/she may have to try several times to make a really big bubble.
  - When he/she's made a bubble, have him/her touch it gently with a wet finger to see what happens.
  - Have him/her make another big bubble, then touch it with a dry finger. What happens?
- Ask him/her to look closely at the bubbles he/she makes. How many colors does he/she see? Do the colors change?

Bubbles are bits of air or gas trapped inside a liquid ball. The surface of a bubble is very thin. Bubbles are particularly fragile when a dry object touches them. That's because soap film tends to stick to the object, which puts a strain on the bubble.

4. Bugs!

Kindergarten - Grade 1

Children can improve their understanding of the natural world and their classification skills by observing bugs.

What Parents Need?

- Books about insects and spiders — preferably with photographs
- A magnifying glass

What Can Parents Do?

- With your child, search your home and neighborhood for bugs. Look for bugs:
  - around your front door
  - in cracks in the sidewalk
  - in gardens
  - at picnic areas
  - on lights
  - in corners of rooms
- Using the books, help your child to identify each type of bug that you find, such as ants, spiders, beetles, crickets, bees, flies, butterflies, mosquitoes, moths, wasps or ladybugs.

- If you find ants, point out that ants work together as a community. Have him/her observe, for example, what an ant does when it finds a bit of food. Explain that when an ant finds food, it doesn't eat it on the spot. It runs back to the hill to "tell" the other ants. As it runs, it leaves a trail that the other ants can smell. These ants can then find the food by smelling their way along the trail.

- Find out about spiders:
    - Why do spiders spin webs?
    - What are webs made of?
    - How many pairs of legs do they have?
- Help your child to think of other ways that he/she might classify the bugs — for example, by color or by size or by whether they have wings or antennae.

Bugs do what they do to survive. They're constantly looking for food. Bugs can be both helpful and harmful. Termites, for example, have a bad reputation because they destroy houses by eating the wood. But termites have a good side, too. In a forest, they break down dead trees, which keeps the forest floor from becoming too cluttered.

5. Float or Sink?

Kindergarten - Grade 1

Learning to make and test predictions is a good first step towards making and testing hypotheses.

What Parents Need?

- 1 block of solid wood
- 1 plastic bottle cap
- 2 pieces of heavy-duty aluminum foil
- 1 piece of modeling clay
- Sink filled with water

What Can Parents Do?

- Tell your child to hold the wood block in one hand and the plastic cap in the other hand. Ask him/her to answer the following questions:
  - Which one feels heavier?
  - Do you think the wooden block will float or sink?
  - Will the plastic cap float or sink?

  Have your child test his predictions by carefully placing the block of wood and the cap on the water. What happens? Next, have him/her put both under the water. What happens now?
- Give him/her a piece of aluminum foil and tell him/her to squeeze it tightly into a solid ball then drop it in the water. Does it float or sink? Give him/her another piece of foil. Help him/her to

shape it into a little boat, then have him/her carefully place it on top of the water. Does the foil float now?

- Help him/her to try the same experiment with the clay. Have him/her make a ball and drop it in the water. What happens? Then have him/her shape the clay into a boat and put it on the water. Does it float now?

The clay and foil balls sink because they are squeezed into small shapes and only a small amount of water is trying to hold up the weight. When the clay or foil is spread out, it floats because the weight is supported by a lot more water.

6. Slime Time

Grades 1-2

When one object moves against another, the result is friction.

What Parents Need?

- Mixing bowl
- 4 envelopes of unflavored gelatin
- Hot water
- Square baking pan
- Vegetable oil
- Liquid dishwashing detergent
- 2 small bowls
- Stopwatch or a watch with a second hand
- Measuring cup

Don't let your child eat the gelatin cubes after they've been handled or after they're covered with lubricant.

What Can Parents Do?

- In a mixing bowl, dissolve the gelatin in two cups of hot tap water. Coat the inside of the pan with vegetable oil. Pour the gelatin mixture into the pan and put it in the refrigerator until firm. Cut the gelatin into cubes about 1 inch x 1 inch. You should have about 64 cubes. Place 15 cubes into one bowl. Place the second bowl about 6 inches (about 15 centimeters) away from the cube bowl. Place the watch so that your child can see it. Tell him/her that when you say go, you want him/her to start picking up the gelatin cubes one at a time with his/her thumb and index finger (caution him/her not to squeeze them!). Tell him/her to see how many cubes he/she can transfer to the other bowl in 15 seconds. Tell your child to put all the cubes back in the first bowl. Pour ¼ cup dishwashing liquid over the cubes. Gently mix the detergent and the cubes so that the cubes are well-coated. Have him/her use the same method as before to transfer as many cubes as possible in 15 seconds.

- Throw away the cubes and detergent and wash and dry both bowls. Put 15 new cubes into one bowl and pour 1/4 cup water over the cubes, again making sure the cubes are thoroughly coated. Tell your child to see how many cubes he/she can transfer in 15 seconds.

- Again, throw away the cubes and water. Put 15 new cubes into one bowl. Pour 1/4 cup of vegetable oil over the cubes. Make sure they are well coated. Have him/her see how many cubes he/she can transfer in 15 seconds.
- Ask your child to answer the following questions:
  - With which liquid was he/she able to transfer the most cubes?
  - With which liquid was he/she able to transfer the fewest cubes?
  - Which liquid was the best lubricant (the slipperiest)? Which was the worst?

Cars, trucks, airplanes and machines all have parts that rub against one another. These parts would heat up, wear down and stop working if we didn't have lubricants. Lubricants reduce the amount of friction between two surfaces that move against each other.

7. Celery Stalks at Midnight

Grades 1-2

Capillary action is the name for the process that takes place when a paper towel soaks up a spilled liquid or when a plant transfers water from its roots to its leaves.

What Parents Need?

- 4 same-size stalks of fresh celery with leaves
- 4 cups of the same size

- Knife
- Vegetable peeler
- Red and blue food coloring
- Measuring cup
- Paper towels
- Ruler
- Old newspapers
- Water

What Can Parents Do?

- Lay the four stalks of celery in a row on a cutting board or counter so that the place where the stalks and the leaves meet matches. Cut all four stalks of celery 4 inches (about 10 centimeters) below where the stalks and leaves meet.
- Use 10 drops of red and 10 drops of blue food coloring for each 1/2 cup of water to make purple water. Pour the colored water in equal parts into the four cups. Have your child put one stalk each in the cups of purple water.
- Label four sheets of paper towels: "2 hours," "4 hours," "6 hours," and "8 hours." (You may want to put newspapers under the towels). Every two hours, have him/her remove one of the stalks and put it on the correct towel.
- Each time he/she removes a stalk from the water, help him/her to carefully peel the rounded part

with a vegetable peeler to see how far up the stalk the purple water has traveled.

- Help your child to measure the distance the purple water has traveled for each stalk and record the information in his/her science journal. Talk with him/her about what he/she has observed.
- Work with your child to make a list of other objects around the house or in nature that illustrates capillary action. Have him/her look for paper towels, sponges, old sweat socks, brown paper bags and flowers.

Capillary action happens when water molecules are more attracted to the surface they travel along than to each other. In paper towels, the molecules move along tiny fibers. In plants, they move through narrow tubes that are actually called capillaries. Plants couldn't survive without capillaries because they use the water to make their food.

8. Icky Sticky Stuff

Grades 2-3

Adhesives are used to stick things together. Many adhesives occur in nature and have important uses for plants and animals.

What Parents Need?

- Flour
- Measuring cup
- Egg white

- Food coloring
- 4 small bowls
- 4 plastic spoons
- Aluminum foil
- Cotton balls
- Toothpicks
- Small pieces of cloth
- Glitter
- Safety scissors
- Colored yarn or ribbon
- Colored paper

What Can Parents Do?

- Help your child to make a poster or collage using adhesives by doing the following:
  - Make three bowls of flour-and-water paste. In each bowl, add 1/4 cup water to 1/2 cup flour and mix until smooth. Add a different-colored food coloring to each of the three bowls and mix. Use the pastes to make colored shapes on a poster board or heavy paper.
  - Crack open an egg and separate the white into a bowl. Use the white as a clear glue to attach aluminum foil, cotton balls, toothpicks, cloth, glitter, ribbon, yarn and colored paper — whatever works to create a collage.

- Help your child to search your home to track down everything that he/she can that is sticky. See how many of the following he/she can find:
  - Tape
  - Peanut butter
  - Postage stamps
  - Envelopes
  - Honey
  - A decal (transfer) on a t-shirt
  - Spackle [powder (containing gypsum plaster and glue] that when mixed with water forms a plastic paste used to fill cracks and holes in plaster)
  - An adhesive bandage
- Ask your child to make a list of things in nature — animals, plants and so forth — that have adhesive properties or are sticky. For example:
  - Spiders that use sticky threads to create webs to catch their food
  - Tree sap
  - Barnacles that stick to boats, ships and rocks
- Next, ask him/her to think of adhesives that are used in hospitals? In offices? In auto repair shops?

What makes glue, paste or tape stick to things? Wood, paper and many other materials have tiny cracks and holes in them. When we glue things together, sometimes the glue seeps into the tiny openings and hardens, making the materials stick together. Other times, the molecules on the surface of an object get tangled up with the glue molecules, making the objects stick together.

9. Splish Splash

Grades 2-3

This activity introduces children to the scientific concepts of *volume* and *measurement.*

What Parents Need?

- Measuring spoons and cups of different sizes
- Milk containers of different sizes — e.g. 1/2 liter, 1 liter, half-gallon (2 liter) and gallon (4 liter)
- Funnel
- 2 containers that hold the same amount but have different shapes — e.g. one tall and thin, one short and squat (try a 1-liter pitcher and the same-sized storage bowl)
- 1 sink filled with water

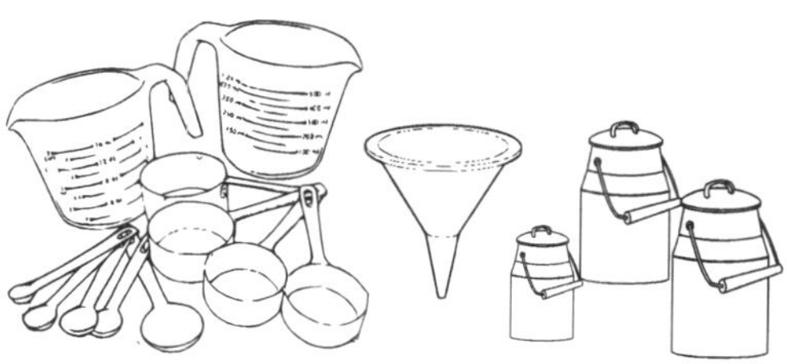

What Can Parents Do?

- Have your child fill a 1 liter container with water. Then help him/her to use the funnel to pour the water into a gallon container. Ask him/her to observe how many small containers it takes to fill the larger one.
- Continue by having him/her use the different measuring devices to answer question such as the following:
    - How many tablespoons does it take to make a milliliters?
    - How many milliliters does it take to make a 1 liter?
    - How many ½ liter make a gallon?
- Set the short 1-liter container next to the tall thin one. Ask your child to predict whether one container will hold more water than the other. Let him/her fill the short 1-liter container with a given amount of water — for example, 1000 milliliters if you're using 1-liter containers. Then have him/her pour this water into the tall thin container. Was his prediction correct? Ask him/her why he/she thinks both containers held the same amount.

Water and other liquids take the shape of whatever container they're in. Containers of certain sizes have names — liter or gallon, for example. This activity provides an introduction to volume and measurement.

10. Hair-Raising Results

Grades 3 and up

Here are some great hands-on ways to learn about static electricity.

What Parents Need?

- A cool dry day
- 2 round balloons (inflated and tied)
- 2 20-inch pieces of string
- Wool or acrylic sock
- Mirror

What Can Parents Do?

- Have your child tie a string to each inflated balloon. Then tell him/her to rub a balloon on his/her hair for about 15 seconds — help him/her to rub around the whole balloon. Have him/her take the balloon away and see what happens to his/her hair! Then have him/her observe what happens when he/she brings the balloon back close to his/her hair.

- Next, stand a few feet away and facing your child. Have him/her rub the balloon on his/her hair again as you do the same with the other balloon. Tell him/her to hold the string to his/her balloon, letting it hang freely but without letting it touch anything. (You do the same with your balloon.) Slowly move the two balloons towards each other, but don't let them touch. Have your child tell you what's happening: Do the balloons push away from each other, or do they pull towards each other? Have him/her place his/her hand between the two hanging balloons. What happens?
- Give your child a sock to place over one hand. Tell him/her to rub his/her balloon with the sock, then let the balloon hang freely. Have him/her move his/her sock-covered hand near the balloon. What happens? Have him/her try rubbing both balloons with the sock and then letting them hang near each other. What happens now?

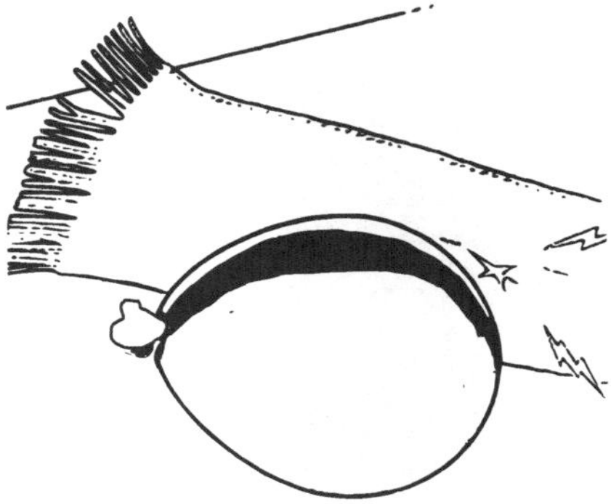

All materials contain millions of tiny particles, called protons and electrons, that have electric charges. Protons have positive charges, and electrons negative ones. Usually, they balance each other, but sometimes when two surfaces rub together, some of the electrons rub off one surface onto the other, and we can have static electricity. Materials with like charges (all positive or all negative) move away from each other; those with opposite charges attract each other.

11. Plants

Grades 3 and up

A few seeds and household plants can teach children about cause and effect and change.

What Parents Need?

- Household plants
- Plant fertilizer
- Paper
- Safety scissors
- A magnifying glass
- Seeds
- Permanent markers: green, red, blue, black
- Paper towels
- Water
- Sandwich bags (without zip locks)

What Can Parents Do?

- With your child, take two clippings from one houseplant. Have him/her put one clipping in a glass of water and the other clipping in a glass without water. Tell him/her to check each day to observe and record how long the one without water can survive.

- Have your child water all of the plants for several weeks. In addition, have him/her choose one or two of the plants to fertilize during this time. Have him/her label the plants to be fertilized. Tell him/her to record the following in his/her science journal:

    - Did any of the plants start to droop?
    - Did any of the plants have yellow leaves that fell off?
    - Did any of the plants grow towards the light?

- Next, have your child observe what happens when a plant (or part of a plant) doesn't get any light. Help him/her to do the following:

    - Cut out three pieces of paper, each about 2 inches x 2 inches in size.
    - Clip the pieces to different leaves of a plant, preferably one that has large leaves.
    - Leave one piece of paper on a leaf for one day, a second for two days and a third for a week.

Ask your child to record how long it takes for the plant to react and how long it takes for the plant to return to normal once the paper is removed.

- To show your child how seeds germinate, have him/her divide some seeds of the same kind into four equal batches. Tell him/her to spread each batch of seeds on a wet paper towel folded into quarters, and then put each batch into a separate sandwich bag. Give him/her the markers and tell him/her to color one bag red, one green, one yellow and one black. Have him/her put the bags in the sun for a week. Tell him/her to check each day to make sure the paper towels are still wet.

  After a week, have him/her examine the bags. Ask him/her which color light was the best for seed germination.

  Ask your child to explore what other things can make seeds germinate faster. Have him/her, for example, put a little soapy water on one batch of seeds and clear water on another.

Photosynthesis means to "make food using light." Plants use sunlight to turn carbon dioxide from the air and water into food. When the plant gets enough food, it produces a simple sugar, which it uses immediately or stores in a converted form of starch. We don't know exactly how this happens. But we do know that chlorophyll, the green substance in plants, helps it to occur.

12. Crystals

Grades 4 and 5

A crystal is a special kind of solid. Growing crystals introduces children to change and variation.

What Parents Need?

- A magnifying glass
- Table salt
- Epsom salt
- Honey container
- Measuring cups and spoons
- Paper cut into circles
- Safety scissors
- Pencil

What Can Parents Do?

- Help your child to use a magnifying glass to look for crystals. Inspect the table salt, Epsom salt and honey container (particularly if it has been open for awhile). Ask your child to draw pictures in his/her journal of what he/she observes. Do all of the crystals look the same? If not, how are they different?

- Have your child try dissolving salt crystals and forming new ones. Help him/her to do the following:
  - Dissolve 1 teaspoon of salt in 1 cup of water.
  - Heat the mixture over low heat to evaporate the water.

What's left? What shape are these crystals?

- Snowflakes are made of ice crystals. They're beautiful, but hard to see clearly. Making paper snowflakes will give your child an idea of what snowflakes look like. Have him/her:
  - Take a circle of paper (use thin paper) and fold it in half.
  - Fan-fold it.
  - Make cuts along all the edges.
  - Unfold them.

When certain liquids and gases cool and lose water, crystals are formed. Crystals are made up of molecules that fit neatly together in an orderly package. All crystals of the same material have the same shape, regardless of their size.

13. Let them Make Cake!

All Ages

Making cakes is an enjoyable way to help children of all ages learn about chemical reactions and change.

What Parents Need?

- 3 small bowls
- Several sheets of aluminum foil
- Pie pan
- Cooking oil
- Measuring spoons
- Ingredients for one cake: (You'll need to measure and mix this set of ingredients four times — with the exceptions that are given below).
  - 6 tablespoons flour
  - 3 tablespoons sugar
  - 1 pinch of salt
  - 2 or 3 pinches of baking powder
  - 2 tablespoons milk
  - 2 tablespoons cooking oil
  - 1/4 teaspoon vanilla
  - Part of an egg (Break egg into a cup; beat until mixed. Use 1/3 of it. Save the rest for 2 of the other cakes.)

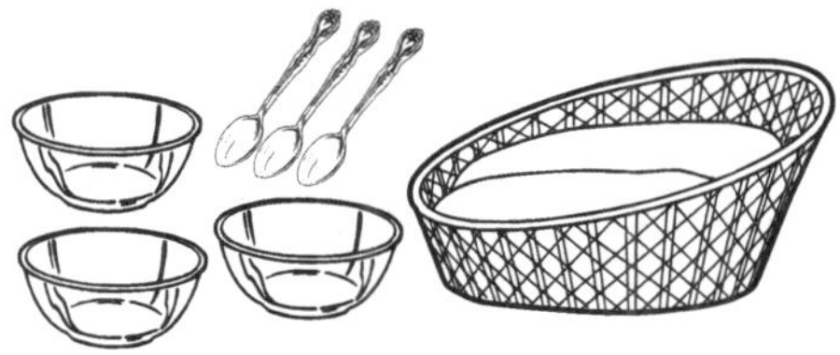

What Can Parents Do?

- With your child do the following:
  - Wrap several sheets of aluminum foil around the outside of a small bowl to form a mold.
  - Remove your foil "pan" and put it in a pie pan for support.
  - Oil the "inside" of the foil pan with cooking oil so the cake doesn't stick.
  - Turn the oven on to 350 degree. <!>
  - Mix all of the dry ingredients together.
  - Add the wet ones (only use 1/3 of the egg; save the rest for later use).
  - Stir the ingredients until smooth and all the same color.
  - Pour batter into the "pan."
  - Bake for 15 minutes.
- Help your child to make three more cakes, but tell him/her to do the following:
  - Leave the oil out of one.
  - Leave the egg out of another.
  - Leave the baking powder out of the third.

- After baking, have him/her cut each cake in half and look inside.
  - Do the cakes look different from each other?
  - Do they taste different from each other?
- Tell your child to write about, or draw pictures of, what he/she observes.

Here are some chemical reactions that occur as a cake bakes:

✓ Heat helps baking powder produce tiny bubbles of gas, which makes the cake light and fluffy (leavening).
✓ Heat causes protein from the egg to change and make the cake firm.
✓Oil prevents the heat from drying out the cake.

xxx

Happiness is when...

you realize your children have turned out to be good people.

6 SCIENCE IN THE COMMUNITY

"Parenting now is a two-way relationship where you learn from each other."
~ *Juhi Chawla*

Our communities offer many opportunities and resources to help children learn science, including

- Zoos;
- Museums;
- Planetariums;
- Aquariums;
- Farms;
- Science at Work;
- Community Science Groups and Organizations; and
- Other Community Resources.

To find out more about resources in your community: Check your local newspaper, a local guidebook or your telephone directory. Or, go online and search the Internet. Other good sources of information and ideas might be your child's teacher, the school librarian or the children's librarian at your local public library. Before you pay a visit to a museum, planetarium, or the like, be sure to check the hours it's open and what cost — if any — is involved. Note that some places may charge entry fees at certain times and grant free admission at other times.

Zoos

Zoos are great places for you to encourage your child's interest in the natural world and to introduce him/her to exotic animals that he/she might not otherwise ever see. Here are a few suggestions to help make your visit to a zoo worthwhile:

Discuss expectations with your child. What does he/she think he/she'll find at the zoo? A very young or insecure child may go to the zoo with a more positive attitude if you assure him/her that it has food stands, water fountains and washrooms.

Don't try to see everything in one visit. Zoos are such busy places that they can overwhelm children, particularly pre-schoolers and kindergarteners. Usually, it is so big that your child will get tired if you will try to make him see everything.

Try to visit zoos at off hours or times of the year (very early on a Saturday morning, for example, or in winter). Choosing less crowded times to visit will allow your child unobstructed views of the animals, as well as a more leisurely tour of the exhibits.

Look for special programs that are set up just for children. Try to search for some special programs such as petting zoos, exploring local habitats and getting involved with conservation projects. Such programs provide children with hands-on opportunities that are otherwise prohibited by most zoos and allow families to learn about wildlife by getting involved in conservation efforts and exploring local habitats together.

As you tour the zoo, keep your child interested and focused. Try the following activities:

- **Play a guessing game.** Guessing games can help your child understand form and function. You might, for example, ask questions such as the following:
    - Why do you think Otters have flippers? (Otters use flippers to swim through the water).

- Why do you think these langoors have such long, strong arms? (Their arms help them swing through the trees).
- Why does that tortoise have a shell that looks like it's covered with armor? Why is its body covered with this shell? (The shell protects it from other animals that want to eat or kill it).
- Why is that snake is of the same brown color as the ground? (As snakes evolved, the brown ones didn't get eaten as quickly).

- **Match the animals**. Children can learn about organization by seeing related animals. Have them compare the sizes, leg shapes, feet, ears, claws, feathers or scales of various creatures. Ask them, "Does the lion look like a regular cat?" "How are they the same?" "Does the gorilla look like the baboon?" (Caution: Take time to read any signs that provide descriptions and classifications of animals and use this information in your discussions. Dolphins, for example, are not fish; they're mammals. Asking children to compare a dolphin to a shark might reinforce children's wrong ideas).

As your child gets older, he/she will understand more complex answers to these questions.

After the visit, have your child do follow-up activities and projects. A child who particularly liked the flamingos and ducks may enjoy building a birdhouse for the backyard. One who liked the mud turtle may enjoy using a margarine tub as a base for making a papier-mâché turtle.

Museums

In museums, both you and your child can have fun and learn science together. Science and technology museums, natural history museums and children's museums can be found in many middle-sized and smaller communities, as well as in large cities.

Museums vary in quality. If possible, try to find museums that have special areas, exhibits and "hands-on" programs just for children. In these programs, children are often able to use scientific equipment that is far too expensive or specialized for their schools to own. Look for museums that have:

- Levers to pull;
- Lights to switch on;
- Buttons to push;
- Animals to stroke; and
- Experiments to do.

Many museums offer special science classes. These enable visitors to see giant-screen movies on subjects ranging from space launches to exploring the Antarctic.

Many of the tips for visiting the zoo are also helpful when you visit museums. For example, don't try to cover too much on one visit, and do try visiting at off hours when the crowds won't seem overwhelming.

Planetariums

Planetariums have wonderful exhibits and activities for youngsters. There are about 35 major planetariums in India, ranging from small ones that hold about 20 people to giant facilities with hundreds of seats. These facilities are particularly useful for children who live in urban areas, where city lights and air pollution obstruct the view of the sky.

Inside a planetarium, your child may be able to:

- use a telescope to view the rings of Saturn;
- see details of the "sky" from inside the planetarium's dome; and

- step on scales to learn what he/she would weigh on the moon or on Mars.

Aquariums

Aquariums enable youngsters to see all kinds of marine life, from starfish to electric eels, and to learn about their special habitats. There are some shark species that seen to do okay in aquariums. Your child can see a lot of nurse sharks, zebra sharks, and tiger sharks in aquarium.

Your child may particularly enjoy feeding times. Before visiting an aquarium, call ahead to find out when the coral fishes, red-tail sharks and other creatures get to eat. Also check for special shows that feature marine life.

Farms

A visit to a farm can be a wonderful trip for you and your child. If you don't know any farmer, ask for a referral from your state extension office, farm bureau or local agriculture office.

If you visit a dairy farm, encourage your child to ask questions about the cows and their care. What do they eat? Do they sleep? Where is their food kept? What happens to the milk when it leaves the farm? How does it get to the grocery store? Many dairy farmers will let your child try him/her hand at milking a cow; others will explain how the equipment is used and the way milk makes its way from the farm to the grocery shelf.

If you visit a farm that grows crops, encourage your child to look at the crops and ask questions about what he/she sees. What crops are grown? How are they planted? How are they harvested? What are they used for? How do they get to the grocery store? If your child grew up in a city, he/she may have no idea what corn, soybeans, potatoes or pumpkins look like as they grow in a field. *(Caution: Don't let your child eat vegetables of fruit unless they have been carefully washed — and the farmer has given permission!).*

On any kind of farm, farmers use special machines such as tractors, harvesters, balers and so forth. Encourage your child to ask about any machines that he/she sees, including what they're used for and how they work.

Science at Work

Your child may recognize that many people use science to do their jobs — chemists, doctors, science teachers, computer technicians and engineers, for example. However, he/she may not realize that many other jobs also require science skills.

To show your child how important science is for many jobs, try to arrange for him/her to spend part of a day — or even an hour — with a park ranger, pharmacist, veterinarian, electrician, plumber, dry cleaner, mechanic, architect, mason or anyone else whose job involves some kind of science. You may also ask your child to watch his mother cooking in the kitchen. Mind cooking does also involve science.

Before any visit, encourage your child to read about the job so that he/she'll be able to ask good questions. For example, he/she might ask a dry cleaner questions such as the following:

- What chemicals do you use to clean clothes?
- How are stains removed?
- What happens to the chemicals after you use them?

Community Science Groups and Organizations

Many communities have groups and organizations that include science programs as part of their services for children. Some may sponsor local summer science camps — focusing on areas that range from computers and technology to natural science to space. Check out, for example:

- the Boy Scouts, Girl Scouts, or similar groups;
- YMCAs and YWCAs; or
- local colleges and universities.

Other Community Resources

Botanical gardens, weather stations, hospital laboratories, sewage treatment plants, newspaper plants, recycling centers, and radio and television stations are only a few of the kinds of places in your community where your child can learn more about all kinds of science. Try the following:

Arrange a tour of a recycling center or landfill to show your child what happens to the community's trash. Before the visit, ask him/her to think about questions such as the following:

- Where does the trash go when it leaves our home?
- What happens to it?
- How much trash does our community produce each year?

- What kinds of materials are recycled?
- What kinds of things can't be recycled?

As you tour the facility, have your child ask the questions; then compare his/her earlier thoughts to what he/she has learned.

Contact your local water department or sewage treatment center to arrange a tour of its facilities. Before the visit, ask your child to think about where the water comes from that he/she drinks and where it goes when it has been used. Is anything added to the water to make it safe to drink? Does all the water used in the community come from the same place? Does all the sewage in the community go to the same place? What happens to the sewage? Again, have him/her compare his/her earlier answers to what he/she learns on the tour.

Finally don't overlook your local public library as a rich resource for books and magazines on science; videos and DVDs; free Internet access; special programs — such as book talks — that relate to science and much more.

xxx

"The voice of parents is the voice of gods, for to their children they are heaven's lieutenants." ~William Shakespeare

7 WORKING WITH TEACHERS AND SCHOOLS

"The true character of a society is revealed in how it treats its children."
~ *Nelson Mandela*

Research has shown that children at all grade levels do better in school, feel more confident about themselves as learners and have higher expectations for themselves when their parents are supportive of and involved with their education. Here are some ways through which you can stay involved in your child's school life:

Visit your child's school. During your visit, look for clues as to whether the school values science.

- Do you see science learning centers? Displays related to science? Science-related drawings on the bulletin boards? Are there plants, terrariums, aquariums or collections (of rocks or insects, for example) in the classrooms, front hall or library?

- Do you see any science equipment in evidence? Are there magnifiers? Magnets? Pictures? Videos? Is the equipment up-to-date?
- Does the school library contain science books? If so, are they latest?
- Is there enough space in the classrooms or elsewhere in the school for students to conduct science experiments?

Find out about the school's science curriculum. Ask for a school handbook. If none is available, meet with the school's principal and ask questions such as the following:

- What methods and materials does the school use for science instruction? Are these methods based on sound research evidence about what works best? Are the materials up-to-date? Can students do hands-on science projects? Does the science curriculum follow state science standards and guidelines?
- Are the science teachers qualified enough? Do they meet state certification and subject-area knowledge requirements?
- How much time is spent on science instruction?
- How does the school measure student progress in science? What tests does it use?

- How do the students at the school score on state assessments of science?
- Are activities available that parents can use at home to supplement and support instruction?

Meet with your child's teacher. Schedule an appointment and ask how your child approaches science. Does he/she enjoy it? Does he/she participate actively? Does he/she understand assignments and do them accurately? If the teacher indicates that your child has problems with science, ask for specific things that you can do to help him/her.

Visit your child's classroom. In the classroom, look for the following:

- Do students have opportunities for hands-on experiences working with materials? Do students discuss their ideas, make predictions and offer explanations? Do they have opportunities to talk and work with each other as well as with the teacher?

- Does the instruction show students how to connect the science concepts they're learning to their personal experiences and to explore how science and technology affect their lives?
- Does instruction include activities in which students apply their science skills and knowledge to real problems and situations?
- Do students have opportunities to use science equipment and technology?
- Does the teacher expect all students to succeed? Does he/she help them set high goals for themselves? Does he/she listen to their explanations and ideas?
- Do science tests and assessments match state and local standards? Do they match what has been taught? Are they used appropriately to plan instruction and evaluate students' understanding?

Find out if the school has a website and, if so, get the address. School websites can provide you with ready access to all kinds of information, including homework assignments, class schedules, lesson plans and test dates.

Find out how your child's school is performing. Check the performance of your child's school by checking its annual report card. Prepared by your school district, this report card shows how students at your school performed on state assessments and how their performance compares to that of other schools in the district.

Get actively involved. Attend parent-teacher meetings. If you're unable to attend, ask that the minutes of the meetings be sent to you, or that they be made available on the school's website. If your schedule permits, volunteer to help with the science program. Teachers often send home lists of ways in which parents can get involved, including the following:

- Assisting with classroom science projects;
- Chaperoning science-related field trips;
- Offering to set up a science display in the school's front hallway or in your child's classroom;
- Leading hands-on lessons (if you have a good science background yourself);
- Helping in a computer laboratory or other area requiring adult supervision; and
- Starting a drive to raise money for computers, science equipment, books or field trips.

Even if you can't volunteer for work at the school, you can help your child learn when you're at home and contribute a great deal to his/her success at school. The key question is, "What can I do at home, easily and in a few minutes each day, to reinforce and extend what the school is teaching?"

xxx

RESOURCES

"Children are our second chance to have a great parent-child relationship."
~ Laura Schlessinger

Resources for Science are a great tool for helping your kids get interest in science, experiment and develop the analytical ways of thinking. These resources will also make them inquisitive about the things happening around them and find the answers of all those that require the knowledge of science.

Books for Children

Libraries and bookstores now have an enormous number of excellent science-related books for children. When making selections, you may want to consider questions that the teachers use in evaluating books. For instance:

- Does the author have a good science background and reputation?
- Is the content interesting to children?
- Is the sequence of events logical?
- Is the format (the placement of pictures, photographs and text) pleasant and easy to follow?
- Are the pictures, photographs and illustrations accurate, and do they match the text?
- Is the vocabulary appropriate? (Big words are OK if they are explained and used in context).
- Are the suggested activities safe? Practical?

When selecting books, also keep in mind:

- Children can learn science from "non-science" books too, such as fictional stories, biographies and historical accounts.
- Recommended age or grade levels are usually printed on a book's back cover, but they are

recommendations only. You're the best judge of which books are appropriate for your child, regardless of age. Just take special care with age-level recommendations for those books that could pose potential safety hazards, such as the use of certain equipment or chemicals.

Science Toys

Children don't need fancy science toys or kits to learn science. However, if you want to buy them for your child, you'll find that toy stores, hobby shops and science specialty shops have a large selection of kits and toys to choose from. It's beyond the scope of this book to recommend specific toys. However, the following tips can guide you in making good choices:

- Make sure that the toy you choose matches your child's interests. If he/she's interested in animals and how they live, he/she may not benefit from — or use — a chemistry kit.

- Learn what the toy can and cannot do before you buy it. If your child is interested in astronomy, he/she may be dis-appointed if he/she looks through the toy telescope you gave him/her and finds out he/she can't see bumps and craters on the moon.
- Make sure the toy is appropriate for your child's age group. Toys that are too complicated — or too simple — can frustrate or bore children.
- Read the instructions that come with the toy carefully so that you understand how it works and how it should be used.

Science on TV

Even though the quality of the science programming seen on TV varies a lot, some programs are able to provide accurate science information in a way that both informs children and captures and holds their interest.

Good science programs can be found on broadcast networks, on cable or satellite channels (such as the Discovery Channel, the National Geographic Channel, Nickelodeon and the Disney Channel), as well as on public television stations. To find the best programs for your child, ask his/her science teacher to make recommendations or check your local listings.

Children can learn science from other TV programs as well. For example, as you watch TV with your child, call his/her attention to news stories that involve scientific discoveries or scientists. Have his/her identify characters on favorite TV shows that have science-related jobs, such as emergency medical personnel, pharmacists or engineers.

If you watch science-fiction programs, talk with him/her about the science involved — Is it accurate? What different kinds of science can she identify? If you watch sports events, ask him/her how science plays a part in the things athletes do — throwing a football, hitting a baseball or tennis ball, kicking a soccer ball. For cooking shows, talk with him/her about the changes and chemical reactions that take place while preparing a meal. The possibilities are endless!

If possible, record some of your own favorite science programs so that you and your child can watch them together. Stop — or replay — parts of the program that are particularly interesting or hard to understand and talk with him/her about what is happening.

Science on the Internet

Through the Internet, your child can have access to a vast array of science resources. Many of these resources are both educational and entertaining. Others, however, are inappropriate for children or provide inaccurate information. Here are some suggestions for helping your child use Internet resources appropriately:

- Monitor your child's use of the Internet by visiting websites with him/her. Check the kinds of information available to see if it is age-appropriate and the activities to see if they are dangerous or inaccurate.
- Look into software or online services that filter out offensive materials and sites. Options include stand-alone software that can be installed on your computer and devices that label or filter content directly on the Web. In addition, many Internet Service Providers and commercial online services offer site blocking, restrictions on incoming e-mail and children's accounts that access specific services. Many of these can be obtained for free or for modest costs at your local electronics store.
- Make sure that your child knows not to give out personal information over the computer, such as his phone number or computer password.
- Help your child to tell the difference between "real" science activities and information and advertisements for toys, kits and games.

Websites

The following websites are some of the many that contain great links for both you and your child, in addition to the Government websites. Most of these listings provide information about how to search for specific information and links to other age-appropriate sites for children.

- Annenberg/CPB Math and Science Project: www.learner.org/
- Family Education Network: http://fen.com
- The National Museum: http://www.nationalmuseumindia.gov.in/services-for-children
- National Aeronautics and Space Administration (NASA) www.nasa.gov/kidsclub/index.html
- National Geographic Society: http://kids.nationalgeographic.com
- National Wildlife: http://www.wildlifeindia.co.uk/
- A Science Odyssey: www.pbs.org/wgbh/aso/

- Smithsonian Institution: www.si.edu/kids/

Science Camps

Camps that focus on many different fields of science and technology are available across the country for children of elementary school age and up. Some of the organizations listed in the section above may provide information. In addition, check the following:

- NIST (http://www.nist.edu/inspire/index.html) runs ecology camps in various locations.
- The YMCA and YWCA (check for local addresses) hold a variety of camps, including computer camps, for both boys and girls.
- Homi Bhabha Center for Science Education (http://www.hbcse.tifr.res.in/events).

Your child's science teacher, school counselor or the children's librarian at your local public library may be able to help you locate the names and contact information for both local and national science camps.

Understand your Child: Teen and Child Personality Test

http://www.personalitylab.org/tests/ccq_parent_choose.htm

xxx

The best security blanket a child can have is parents who respect each others.

-Jane Blaustone